Charles Péguy

GOD SPEAKS

RELIGIOUS POETRY

TRANSLATION AND
INTRODUCTION BY
Julian Green

PANTHEON

FIRST PRINTING JULY 1945
SECOND PRINTING FEBRUARY 1950
THIRD PRINTING NOVEMBER 1957

LIBRARY OF CONGRESS CATALOG CARD NO.: 57–14419

MANUFACTURED IN THE UNITED STATES OF AMERICA

AB

CONTENTS

INTRODUCTION

BY *Julian Green*

The Life

CHARLES PÉGUY was born on January 7, 1873, at Orléans, the city where Bishop Saint Aignan stopped Attila in the fifth century and where Joan of Arc rallied the forces of France one thousand years later. There was nothing very exalted about Péguy's family. His mother made a hard living by mending chairs, after her husband's death which occurred when their son was still a baby. Péguy was very proud of his humble origins and when he was a grown man with college degrees and one of the masterpieces of French literature among his manuscripts, he was fond of helping his mother mend her chairs and boasted that he did it as well as anyone in the land. He called himself a peasant and insisted that French peasantry represented what was best in France. When an old French peasant speaks, the race itself speaks through his lips, and the nearer you are to that peasant, the nearer you are to the heart of real France. So reasoned Péguy.

When he was twelve, he was sent to the Lycée at Orléans as a scholarship student, and in 1891, having passed both his baccalaureate examinations, he went to Paris in order to prepare for the Ecole Normale. From what he said in later years, it appears that at this period of his life he had lost all belief in the immortality of the soul. He entered the Lycée Lakanal (at Sceaux, in the suburbs of Paris) and one year later failed in his entrance examinations for the Ecole Normale. Possibly as a result of this setback, he decided to enlist, that is, he joined the colors a year before he would normally have been required to do so.

In 1893, he was free from military obligations and, with the Ecole Normale still in his mind, he entered the Lycée Sainte-Barbe, one of the oldest schools in Paris and attended in its early days by such distinguished men as John Calvin and Saint Ignatius Loyola. It was at Sainte-Barbe that Péguy met some of the men who were most helpful to him in later times. There was something so compelling about his personality that the more serious of the students in his class came instinctively to him, as if for guidance.

He was on the small side but very robust and a little heavily built. His brown eyes had a way of suddenly flashing when ideas struck him, they were the bold, forceful eyes of a master. His beautiful and delicately formed hands crushed your own in their powerful grasp. When he spoke, there was immediate silence and everyone listened. Why or how this young man of twenty exercised such authority remains as mysterious as genius itself. He was serious to the point of austerity, discountenancing any form of levity such as gambling or drinking, and apparently untouched by carnal desire. There was something of the reformer about him, a gospel-like singleness of heart together with the obstinacy of a peasant and a boundless ability to take pains.

In 1894, he left Sainte-Barbe and entered the Ecole Normale Supérieure where his old friends soon joined him. This school, as will be remembered, was founded in 1795 for the training of university professors.

As time went on, however, Péguy slowly realized that he was not fitted for a university career, probably because he was now conscious of his power as a writer and found it difficult to reconcile the creative urge and the task of teaching. In December 1895, he asked M. Perrot, the director of the Ecole Normale, for a prolonged leave of absence and returned to Orléans with a threefold purpose in mind: to found a socialist center, to learn printing, and to work on his book in more propitious surroundings. By November 1896, at the beginning of the school session, he was back in his room at 'Normale.' But hardly had a few months elapsed when again he walked into M. Perrot's office and asked for another leave of absence. This time, he wanted to marry. M. Perrot was dumbfounded: examinations were practically at hand, and here was Péguy asking for leave of absence to get married. But Péguy insisted that he would come back and pass his examinations the following year. 'You will fail,' prophesied M. Perrot.

Nevertheless, Péguy left school then and there and proposed to the sister of Marcel Baudoin, a very close friend of his who had died in 1896. The marriage took place in October 1897. One month later, faithful to his word, Péguy was back again at 'Normale.' At that time, Henri Bergson was teaching at the old school and so were Joseph Bédier and Romain Rolland. The ideas they expressed were discussed as ideas are always discussed by Frenchmen, feverishly. But apart from that, there were other causes for excitement in the Latin Quarter at the turn of the century. Some years before, the Jewish captain Dreyfus had been arrested on a charge of treason which later turned out to be imaginary. In 1897, the whole case was to be retried. It would take many pages to tell about the Dreyfus case. Suffice it to say that the whole country was being aroused and divided by the issue at stake, dangerously aroused and dangerously divided. Some people contended that, even if Dreyfus were innocent—which they denied—it would be more expedient to condemn him rather than aspersions to be cast on a military tribunal and also because certain military secrets of great importance to the national defense were involved, but there were others, many others, who insisted that, Jew or no Jew (and that had a great deal to do with it), if Dreyfus was innocent, he was to be freed immediately. And of course, Péguy, with his passion for justice, was very loud in clamoring for the Jewish captain's release.

One has the impression, when reading about Péguy's spiritual difficulties, that as early as 1897 he had an inkling of the crisis to come and that he instinctively shrank from it—instinctively but not consciously—as we are all apt to do when we feel that new problems are about to complicate our lives. There were plenty of complications in store for Péguy. To begin with, the socialist revolution had to be brought about. Also, the daily bread had to be earned. Many plans were agitated. Finally, it was decided that a socialist bookshop would be opened with the financial help of Madame Péguy who owned the then rather large sum of 40,000 francs. A store was found and the bookshop solemnly inaugurated in the spring of 1898, May 1st, the day of leftist demonstrations being, of course, chosen as the date of that event.

Four months later, Péguy who was then completing his third year at 'Normale,' failed at his final examinations, exactly as M. Perrot had predicted, and abandoned all plans for a university career.

In 1901, Péguy had set up a publishing firm of his own to bring out a fortnightly publication called *Les Cahiers de la Quinzaine*, each *Cahier* being really a book in itself. To keep these *Cahiers* going meant a fearful financial struggle. Some of them proved difficult reading, even when Péguy wrote the preface, which added considerably to the bulk of the volume. A number of *Cahiers* were entirely filled with Péguy's own words, bold, often indignant words in defense of the working classes and in attacks on our modern world which he hated. But the modern world cared little whether Péguy hated it or not and scarcely knew his name.

One day in September 1908, Péguy had a conversation with his friend Lotte, about his many worries, when all of a sudden his eyes filled with tears and he said: 'I have not told you all. I have found faith again. I am a Catholic.' This was the outcome of a long struggle about which we know practically nothing. What went on in Péguy's soul from the time he declared himself an atheist, around '92 or '93, to the minute when he unburdened his heart to Lotte is a mystery which will probably never be solved. Nor did this conversion mean a simplifying of life's problems for Péguy. On the contrary. Only from the outside do conversions appear to simplify life's problems. A conversion does not mean that the fight is over and that peace will necessarily reign forever. In Péguy's case it meant quite the opposite. To begin with, there was the fact that he had married into a family of staunch unbelievers and that his children, two boys and a girl, were unbaptized, nor would Madame Péguy hear of having them baptized. And, of course, in the eyes of the Church, he and Madame Péguy were not married. So it was impossible for Péguy to live as a Catholic and he did not go to mass. Even to this day, we are not sure that he ever went to communion after his conversion; it is believed that he received the Sacrament a few weeks before he was killed, but his son Marcel states very definitely that this fact cannot be 'historically proved.'

What spiritual agony this must have meant to Péguy, we can only guess, and faintly guess. He prayed incessantly as he walked from one end of Paris to the other, or on the tops of 'omnibuses' with his beads in his hands and tears running down his face. We can be sure that Péguy did not pray like an amateur; he prayed with the obstinate faith of a medieval peasant, and yet here too were difficulties, for instance that sentence in the Lord's prayer in which we beg for forgiveness was a stumbling-block to Péguy who insisted that we do not

forgive those who trespass against us. But the impor-
tant thing was that he had taken the step which leads
from the outer darkness of atheism to the world of
Christ, and the tears that ran down his cheeks may not
always have been tears of grief.

Early in 1910, what Péguy had confidentially told
Lotte was to be publicly avowed in a work which will
no doubt make its author's name last for centuries in
Catholic France. It bore a long title which reminds
one of a heavy granite lintel over an ancient doorway:
'The Mystery of the Charity of Joan of Arc.' Very
few noticed the book, fewer still realized its importance. The 'Mystery' was published as a *Cahier* but
most probably the subscribers did not even cut its
leaves.

The principal theme of this poem (which we might
hesitate to call a play) is the awakening of Joan of
Arc's vocation. Indeed nothing actually happens which
could properly claim the name of action, nor does anything happen in the second and third Mysteries which
followed in 1911 and 1912. On the other hand, it does
not seem possible to describe this work as a philosophical poem, because philosophical poems as a rule are not
without at least a suggestion of boredom or tedious
abstractness which is wholly lacking in Péguy's Mysteries. Péguy shared with Dante the peculiar gift of
clothing the metaphysical with humanity. He had an
eye for the invisible which only the most mystical
among primitives have had before him, because he was
himself a great primitive and there is nothing in literature more suggestive of Dirk Bouts or Rogier van der

Weyden than his vision of Mary following her son up Mount Calvary, in the passage which I have ventured to translate as 'The Passion of Our Lady.'

Almost complete silence greeted these magnificent poems. Nevertheless, Péguy kept on. His forebodings of an early death were more and more frequent and yet, he said, he must not die. There was still a tremendous number of things to be written about.

One year before he was killed, Péguy's faith was put to a test. One of his sons fell desperately ill with typhoid fever and there seemed to be little hope of saving him. Péguy did what a medieval Frenchman would have done, because he was a medieval Frenchman, he spoke earnestly to Our Lady about his unbaptized children, one of whom was in danger of death. He could not look after them. 'I have enormous responsibilities,' he explained to the Queen of Heaven. 'You must do something for my children. I place them in your lap, I give them to you, and now I am going away before you can give them back to me.'

The sick child recovered. Naturally, said Péguy who showed no surprise (he knew how to ask).* However, he had promised Our Lady of Chartres to make a pilgrimage to her church if his child was saved, but he was not in a hurry to redeem his promise; he was never in a hurry about anything. Several months went by, then he put on his heavy shoes, took his stick and started out on foot in the direction of Chartres. There are seventy-two kilometers between Paris and Chartres

---

* *Later his children were baptized. His wife became a Catholic after his death.*

and it took Péguy three days to cover that distance. He left us an account of his pilgrimage in a poem which, by a caprice of fate, brought him something like recognition a few months before he died.

When the war broke out, Péguy was forty-one and should normally have been in the reserve, but to a man of his type, this was simply unacceptable. Early in August, he left for the front with his regiment, having been given the rank of lieutenant. All during the harrowing month of August, the German armies swept through Northern France until they were stopped, in the first week of September, along the river Marne. Péguy's regiment was in the neighborhood of Senlis. On the third of September, they were quartered for a few hours in a deserted convent. Péguy spent that night decorating the altar of Our Lady with flowers which he had picked. On the fourth, he and his men moved on in the direction of Meaux. On the fifth, in the early part of the afternoon, they were in the neighborhood of Villeroy with shells bursting all around them. The men ran a few yards forward, then stopped and threw themselves on the ground to shoot at the already retreating Germans. But Péguy did not lie down. There he stood in his red and blue uniform, a living target in the blazing sun, telling his men to shoot at will, then running ahead of them to lead them on. They all shouted to him to lie down, but he, with an oath, told them to keep on shooting. The last thing he probably saw was the German line wavering and falling back. A bullet struck him in the forehead and he fell with a groan as his men ran to victory.

Blessed are those who died in great battles,
Stretched out on the ground in the face of God,
Blessed are those who died in a just war,
Blessed is the wheat that is ripe and the wheat that is
gathered in sheaves.

Thus wrote Péguy, in 1913, under the dictation of
his prophetic soul.

The Poetry

IT IS NOT EASY to state in a few sentences what Charles Péguy's poetry consists of or, indeed, why it is poetry. Its language is made up of everyday words, words which might sometimes appear almost worn out for having been used so often; yet those are the words which Péguy seems to prefer to all others, those he handles with greatest care, one might almost say: with piety, as if age and hard work had made them more venerable than the rarer words used by the educated. In Péguy's mind, a word is all the more beautiful if it is used by his charwoman, or by the 'bus conductor, or by the man who sweeps the streets of Paris with a large broom that makes a noise like a storm as it drives the dead leaves into the gutter. Péguy himself talks like those people, and he makes God the Father talk like them too. Neither is his thought lowered by such a process. What happens is that the simple language he uses is incredibly exalted and takes on a majesty which can only remind one of the Scriptures.

Such is the medium he uses: plain language so plain that in some unaccountable way it puts so-called literary styles to shame. With these everyday words, what kind of poetry does he write? To begin with, his poetry, on the printed page, looks like poetry, blank verse, modern in its irregularity. But if we read it aloud, it will seem to us that it is really prose cut up into lines of different lengths and that if these lines were to be put together again, we should have excellent prose. However, if we read it again and listen to the sound of it, and stop ever so little at the end of each line, we will catch a rhythm, not exactly the rhythm of speech, but what might be termed the rhythm of thought. And there, I believe, lies the essence of Péguy's poetry.

When his characters are allowed to speak, they make the most of their opportunity. Their conversation is an exchange of monologues. They go into a monologue as one goes into a trance and whatever remains outside of their monologue ceases to exist. Nor do they ever speak as if they expected an interruption or wished to argue their point. They are constantly making a profession of faith, and just as some people think aloud, they believe aloud. Their real audience is the sun and the moon and the stars, earth, man in general and finally the person with whom they may happen to be at the time. However there is nothing vague about these monologues; they are not the ravings of a dreamer; on the contrary, they come from as logical a brain as France ever produced.

Here we have another element in Péguy's poetry, an element which might be called the beauty of his reasoning. Péguy's reasoning goes from the particular to the general with a magnificent sweep which carries one along as only logic can do when it is enlivened by imagination. Its scope is apparently boundless. Like a true poet, Péguy instinctively, and logically, sees 'a world in a grain of sand,' but he is ever ready to patiently trace all the steps from the grain of sand to its cosmic fulfilment, and he enjoys the trip immensely. No poet ever had a keener sense of the poetry of logic. This passionate love of reasoning, which he shares with his race, is probably one of the strongest intellectual links between France and ancient Greece, which France so often resembles, and we can well imagine the pleasure a platonic philosopher would have found in listening to God the Father's monologue on leprosy and mortal sin, surely as serious a monologue as was ever spoken, yet spoken with occasional smiles and sallies and, in one place at least, with an unmistakable wink.

Another characteristic of Péguy's logic is its beautiful emotional quality. It is strong but not unbending, and it has a way of suddenly moving us almost to tears. The heart has its reasons of which reason knows nothing, wrote Pascal, and in Péguy it is not only the head but the heart that reasons, a hard head and a big, generous, human heart.

Turning to the contents of those mammoth poems which Péguy called *Mysteries*, it seems to me that of all the characters involved, God the Father is the most real if, for want of a better term, the word character can be applied to the first person of the Trinity. We sometimes smile when we listen to him, but we are awed. He is never pompous, he never has to remember to be majestic, being majesty itself. He makes us feel like children and somehow he makes us feel a little better, a little more hopeful. He has a way of making clear what seemed irreparably involved in our spiritual life and with one word unties many knots. At the same time he lowers us somewhat in our self-esteem, he makes us a little ashamed, he makes us look a little foolish in our own eyes, but he does so in such a way that we are happier in consequence; he is eminently 'le bon Dieu,' the good Lord.

When God the Father enlarges on the subject of his universe, in the Mystery of the Second Virtue and in the Mystery of the Holy Innocents, he does so with poise and tremendous authority. He is certainly not lyrical. He blends the simplicity and wisdom of an old French peasant with the knowledge and shrewdness of a Church Father. There is something almost over-whelming about his simplicity, because it is the simplicity of truth and the simplicity of real wisdom. When he speaks of the stars, his stars, of the saints, his own saints, of Faith, of Charity, and of his 'little Hope,' he does so quietly, in fact so very quietly that our breath is taken away. It is not enough to say that he is great; he is great beyond any conception that we may have of greatness, he is the Lord, and because he is the Lord he can speak of creation not only with the authority of the creator, but at the same time with the humor and the matter of fact tone of the farmer who talks about his crops. He is immensely good and immensely for-giving; he grieves to punish the wicked; he is for justice with a strong leaning toward mercy; he loves all his children, particularly the French, for reasons which he explains at length.

Whatever this conception of God the Father may be

worth theologically, it bears the stamp of genius and has its origin in the depths of a truly religious heart. The mere attempt to make God the Father deliver long speeches shows courage, and genius is a form of intellectual courage, the courage it takes to allow inspiration to carry one as far as possible, sometimes too far in the eyes of many. In literature as in other fields, the man who is afraid of going too far will never be among the great, and Péguy, with his firm, steady tread and that logical head of his, and his obstinate common sense, Péguy obviously went too far according to the world's method of reckoning distances, that is, he walked straight into the kingdom of Heaven.

It may be interesting at this point to indicate one of the sources of Péguy's inspiration. As we might have guessed, it was liturgical. Like his elder and greater brother, Francis Thompson, Péguy was a careful reader of the Catholic prayer book, that compact little volume which the French call their *paroissien* and which contains much of the spiritual wealth stored up by the Church since the early days of Christianity. He read the missal with the zeal of the convert. In a way he rediscovered it and studied its many pages with an eye which had become disaccustomed to its language. This allowed him to see things which habit kept Catholics of a longer standing from seeing for themselves.

One instance of what I mean is to be found in the ceremony of Holy Saturday, when the paschal candle is blessed and lighted. This ancient rite is known in English-speaking countries as the Blessing of the New Fire. It is as beautiful as it is old and the prayers read on that occasion are permeated with a feeling of happiness and even of exultation which lend them an almost lyrical quality. We expect them at times to break into a hymn, as if the very words called for music. This impression is heightened by a very moving use of repetitions. A few words from these prayers may be quoted here: "This is the Paschal solemnity, in which the true Lamb is slain . . . This is the night in which Thou didst first cause our forefathers to pass through the Red Sea with dry feet. This therefore is the night which purged away the darkness of sinners by the light of the pillar. This is the night which restores to grace and unites in sanctity those that believe in Christ. This is the night in which Christ arose victorious from the grave . . . O wonderful condescension of Thy Mercy towards us! O inestimable affection of charity . . . ! O truly needful sin of Adam, which was blotted out by the death of Christ! O happy fault, that merited so great a Redeemer! O truly blessed night, which alone deserved to know the time and hour in which Christ rose again from the grave! This is the night of which it is written: And the night shall be enlightened as the day; and the night is my light in my enjoyments . . ."

If having listened to the beautiful music of those words, we turn to Péguy and read the last pages of his second Mystery, we can, I believe, catch an echo of the Catholic liturgy in his invocation of night, whom God the Father calls his daughter:

"You, night, are my great sombre light.* I am glad to have created night . . . Night, my most beautiful

* Splendor nocturna, *says the Church.*

invention . . . O night, o my daughter night, the most religious of my daughters, the most devout . . . Night, you are a beautiful invention of my wisdom. Night, o my daughter night, o my silent daughter at Rebecca's well, at the Samaritan woman's well, it is you who draw the deepest water from the deepest well. O night, you who rock all creation to sleep . . . O night, you who wash all wounds . . . At the Samaritan woman's well, you who draw from the deepest well the deepest prayer. O night, o my daughter night, you who know how to hold your peace, o my daughter of the beautiful mantle . . . you who put the Child Jesus to bed every evening in the arms of the very Holy and Immaculate One. O my daughter sparking and sombre, I greet you . . ."

There probably never was a Catholic more thoroughly enamored of the Church than Péguy, and yet he was remarkably free from any kind of bigotry. Bigotry is one of the besetting sins of converts; a bigot is a person who goes about in a sort of mental cage, but Péguy remained a free man until the moment he was killed; he never lost contact with humanity, he loved humanity, he considered himself, to a great extent, his brother's keeper (and as such assumed the right to shout at him and, if necessary, to kick him), nor did he ever lose his magnificent sense of humor. His greatest gift as a man and a poet was that of being able to speak intelligibly to all men, and to help them; his greatest gift was to give.

Julian Green.

God Speaks

RELIGIOUS POETRY

SLEEP

God Speaks:

I DON'T LIKE the man who doesn't sleep, says
   God.
Sleep is the friend of man.
Sleep is the friend of God.
Sleep is perhaps the most beautiful thing I have
   created.
And I myself rested on the seventh day.
He whose heart is pure, sleeps. And he who sleeps
   has a pure heart.
That is the great secret of being as indefatigable
   as a child.
Of having that strength in the legs that a child
   has.
Those new legs, those new souls,
And to begin afresh every morning, ever new,
Like young hope, new hope.
But they tell me that there are men
Who work well and sleep badly.
Who don't sleep. What a lack of confidence in me.
It is almost more serious than if they worked badly
   and slept well.

Than if they did not work but slept, because
    laziness
Is not a greater sin than unrest,
It is not even so great a sin as unrest
And despair and lack of confidence in me.
I am not talking, says God, about those men
Who don't work and don't sleep.
Those men are sinners, to be sure. They have
    what they deserve.
Great sinners. It's their fault for not working.
I am talking about those who work and don't sleep.
I pity them. I am talking about those who work
    and who, in this,
Obey my commandment, poor children.
And who on the other hand lack courage, lack
    confidence, and don't sleep.
I pity them. I have it against them. A little. They
    won't trust me.
Like the child who innocently lies in his mother's
    arms, thus do they not lie
Innocently in the arms of my Providence.
They have the courage to work. They lack the
    courage to be idle.
They have enough virtue to work. They haven't
    enough virtue to be idle.
To stretch out. To rest. To sleep.
Poor people, they don't know what is good.
They look after their business very well during
    the day.

But they haven't enough confidence in me to let
   me look after it during the night.
As if I wasn't capable of looking after it during
   one night.
He who doesn't sleep is unfaithful to Hope.
And it is the greatest infidelity.
Because it is infidelity to the greatest Faith.
Poor children, they conduct their business with
   wisdom during the day.
But when evening comes, they can't make up
   their minds,
They can't be resigned to trust my wisdom for the
   space of one night
With the conduct and the governing of their
   business.
As if I wasn't capable, if you please, of looking
   after it a little.
Of watching over it.
Of governing and conducting, and all that kind of
   stuff.
I have a great deal more business to look after,
   poor people, I govern creation, maybe that is
   more difficult.
You might perhaps, and no harm done, leave your
   business in my hands, O wise men.
Maybe I am just as wise as you are.
You might perhaps leave it to me for the space of
   a night.
While you are asleep

At last

And the next morning you might find it not too
    badly damaged perhaps.

The next morning it might not be any the worse
    perhaps.

I may yet be capable of attending to it a little. I am
    talking of those who work

And who in this obey my commandment.

And don't sleep, and who in this

Refuse all that is good in my creation,

Sleep, all the good I have created,

And also refuse my commandment just the same.

Poor children, what ingratitude towards me

To refuse such a good

Such a beautiful commandment.

Poor children, they follow human wisdom.

Human wisdom says Don't put off until tomorrow

What can be done the very same day.

But I tell you that he who knows how to put off
    until tomorrow

Is the most agreeable to God.

He who sleeps like a child

Is also he who sleeps like my darling Hope.

And I tell you Put off until tomorrow

Those worries and those troubles which are
    gnawing at you today

And might very well devour you today.

Put off until tomorrow those sobs that choke you

When you see today's unhappiness.

Those sobs which rise up and strangle you.
Put off until tomorrow those tears which fill your
    eyes and your head,
Flooding you, rolling down your cheeks, those
    tears which stream down your cheeks.
Because between now and tomorrow, maybe I,
    God, will have passed by your way.
Human wisdom says: Woe to the man who puts
    off what he has to do until tomorrow.
And I say Blessed, blessed is the man who puts off
    what he has to do until tomorrow.
Blessed is he who puts off. That is to say Blessed is
    he who hopes. And who sleeps.

ABANDONMENT

God Speaks:

I KNOW MAN WELL. It is I who made him. A
  funny creature.
For in him that freedom is at work which is the
  mystery of mysteries.
You can still ask a lot of him. He is not too bad.
  You can't say that he is bad.
When you know how to handle him, you can
  still ask a lot of him.
You can get a lot out of him. And God knows that
  my grace
Knows how to handle him, that with my grace
I know how to handle him, that my grace is
  insidious, as clever as a thief
And like a man hunting a fox.
I know how to handle him. It's my business. And
  that freedom of his is my creation.
You can ask a lot of kindness of him, a lot of
  charity, a lot of sacrifice.
He has much faith and much charity.
But what you can't ask of him, by gum, is a little
  hope.

A little confidence, don't you know, a little
relaxation.
A little yielding, a little abandonment into my
hands,
A little giving in. He is always so stiff.
Now you, my daughter night, you sometimes
succeed, you sometimes obtain that very thing
Of rebellious man.
Let the gentleman consent, let him yield a little to
me.
Let him stretch out his poor weary limbs on a bed
of rest.
Let him ease his aching heart a little on a bed of
rest.
Above all, let his head stop working. It works only
too much, his head does. And he thinks it is
work, when his head goes that way.
And his thoughts . . . Did you ever . . . What
he calls his thoughts!
Let his thoughts stop moving about and struggling
inside his head and rattling like calabash seeds,
Like a little bell in an empty gourd.
When you see what they are all about, those ideas
of his, as he calls them!
Poor creature. I don't care for the man who doesn't
sleep, says God.
The man who is all aglow in his bed, all aglow with
unrest and fever.

I am all for making one's examination of conscience
    every night, says God.

It is a good exercise.

But after all, you mustn't torment yourself with it
    to the point of losing your sleep.

At that hour, the day is done, and well done. It
    doesn't have to be done over again.

It is all settled.

Those sins for which you are so sorry, my boy,
    well, it is plain enough,

My friend, you should not have committed them.

At the time when you were still free not to commit
    them.

Now it's over. So go to sleep, you won't do it again
    tomorrow.

But the man who, going to bed at night, makes
    plans for the next day,

That man I don't care for.

Jackass, how does he know what tomorrow will
    be like?

Does he even know what color the weather is
    going to take on?

He had much better say his prayers. I have never
    withheld tomorrow's bread.

The man who is in my hand like the staff in the
    traveller's hand,

That man is agreeable to me, says God.

The man who rests on my arm like the suckling
    child who laughs

34

And is not concerned with anything,
And sees the world in his mother's and his nurse's
  eyes,
And sees it nowhere else, and looks for it nowhere
  else,
That one is agreeable to me, says God.
But the one who concocts plans, the one who inside
  himself, in his own head,
Works for tomorrow like a hired laborer,
Works dreadfully like a slave making an everlasting
  wheel go round,
(And between you and me like a fool),
Well, that man is in no way agreeable to me, says
  God.
He who abandons himself, I love. He who does not
  abandon himself, I don't love. That's simple
  enough.
He who abandons himself does not abandon
  himself, and he is the only one who does not
  abandon himself.
He who does not abandon himself, abandons
  himself, and is the only one who does abandon
  himself.
Now you, my daughter night, my daughter of the
  great cloak, my daughter of the silver cloak,
You are the only one who sometimes overcomes
  that rebel and can bend that stiff neck of his.
It is then, O night, that you appear.
And what you have done once,

You do every time.
What you have done one day,
You do every day.
As you came down one evening,
So you come down every evening.
What you did for my son who was made man,
O great and charitable one, you do for all men his
    brothers,
You bury them in silence and shadow
And in the salutary oblivion
Of the mortal unrest
Of day.

FREEDOM

God Speaks:

WHEN YOU LOVE SOMEONE, you love him
    as he is.
I alone am perfect.
It is probably for that reason
That I know what perfection is
And that I demand less perfection of those poor
    people.
I know how difficult it is.
And how often, when they are struggling in their
    trials,
How often do I wish and am I tempted to put my
    hand under their stomachs
In order to hold them up with my big hand
Just like a father teaching his son how to swim
In the current of the river
And who is divided between two ways of thinking.
For on the one hand, if he holds him up all the time
    and if he holds him up too much,
The child will depend on this and will never learn
    how to swim.

But if he doesn't hold him up just at the right
    moment
That child is bound to swallow more water than is
    healthy for him.
In the same way, when I teach them how to swim
    amid their trials
I too am divided by two ways of thinking.
Because if I am always holding them up, if I hold
    them up too often,
They will never learn how to swim by themselves.
But if I don't hold them up just at the right
    moment,
Perhaps those poor children will swallow more
    water than is healthy for them.
Such is the difficulty, and it is a great one.
And such is the doubleness itself, the two faces of
    the problem.
On the one hand, they must work out their
    salvation for themselves. That is the rule.
It allows of no exception. Otherwise it would not
    be interesting. They would not be men.
Now I want them to be manly, to be men and to
    win by themselves
Their spurs of knighthood.
On the other hand, they must not swallow more
    water than is healthy for them,
Having made a dive into the ingratitude of sin.
Such is the mystery of man's freedom, says God,

38

And the mystery of my government towards him
    and towards his freedom.
If I hold him up too much, he is no longer free
And if I don't hold him up sufficiently, I am
    endangering his salvation.
Two goods in a sense almost equally precious.
For salvation is of infinite price.
But what kind of salvation would a salvation be
    that was not free?
What would you call it?
We want that salvation to be acquired by himself,
Himself, man. To be procured by himself.
To come, in a sense, from himself. Such is the
    secret,
Such is the mystery of man's freedom.
Such is the price we set on man's freedom.
Because I myself am free, says God, and I have
    created man in my own image and likeness.
Such is the mystery, such the secret, such the price
Of all freedom.
That freedom of that creature is the most beautiful
    reflection in this world
Of the Creator's freedom. That is why we are so
    attached to it,
And set a proper price on it.
A salvation that was not free, that was not, that
    did not come from a free man could in no wise
    be attractive to us. What would it amount to?

What would it mean?

What interest would such a salvation have to offer?

A beatitude of slaves, a salvation of slaves, a
slavish beatitude, how do you expect me to be
interested in that kind of thing? Does one care
to be loved by slaves?

If it were only a matter of proving my might, my
might has no need of those slaves, my might
is well enough known, it is sufficiently known
that I am the Almighty.

My might is manifest enough in all matter and in
all events.

My might is manifest enough in the sands of the
sea and in the stars of heaven.

It is not questioned, it is known, it is manifest
enough in inanimate creation.

It is manifest enough in the government,

In the very event that is man.

But in my creation which is endued with life, says
God, I wanted something better, I wanted
something more.

Infinitely better. Infinitely more. For I wanted that
freedom.

I created that very freedom. There are several
degrees to my throne.

When you once have known what it is to be loved
freely, submission no longer has any taste.

All the prostrations in the world

Are not worth the beautiful upright attitude of a

free man as he kneels. All the submission, all
the dejection in the world
Are not equal in value to the soaring up point,
The beautiful straight soaring up of one single
invocation
From a love that is free.

This poem is based on a passage from Joinville's History of Saint Louis. *The king of France and his baron Joinville were talking one day of leprosy, not an uncommon subject in thirteenth century conversations, and Joinville declared that his horror of that disease was such that he would prefer committing thirty mortal sins rather than become a leper. Whereupon Saint Louis gently reproved him and said that it were better to be a leper than to commit one mortal sin. This is what God the Father has to say on the subject.*

MORTAL SIN AND LEPROSY

God Speaks:

HAVING ONCE KNOWN what it is to be loved
    freely, one no longer finds any flavor in
    submissions.
When one has known what it means to be loved
    by free men, the prostrations of slaves no longer
    please.
When one has seen Saint Louis on his knees, one
    no longer wishes to see
Those Oriental slaves lying prone on the ground
At body's length, on their stomachs, on the ground.
    To be loved freely,
Nothing weighs as much as that weighty thing,

nothing weighs as much as that thing of great
    price,
It is certainly my greatest invention.
Once one has tasted
What it is to be loved freely
All the rest is no more than submissions.
That is why, says God, we are so fond of those
    Frenchmen,
And why, among all other people, we love them
    in an unparalleled way,
And why they will always be my eldest sons.
They have freedom in their blood. Everything
    they do, they do freely.
They are less slavish and freer in sin itself
Than the others in their exercises. Through them
    we have tasted,
Through them we have invented, through them
    we have created
This thing: to be loved by free men. When Saint
    Louis says that he loves me,
I know that he loves me,
At least I know that that one loves me, because he
    is a French baron. Through them we have
    known
What it is to be loved by free men. All the
    prostrations in the world
Are not worth the beautiful upright kneeling of a
    free man. All the submissions, all the
    self-abasements in the world

Are not worth a beautiful prayer, an upright,
    kneeling prayer of those free men. All the
    submissions in the world
Are not worth the soaring point
The beautiful straight soaring of a single invocation
Of a free love. When Saint Louis loves me, says
    God, I am sure,
I know what is meant. He is a free man, he is a
    free baron of the Ile de France. When Saint
    Louis loves me
I am aware, I know what it is to be loved.
(Now that is everything.) No doubt he fears God,
But with a noble fear, all filled, all swollen,
All replete with love, like a fruit swollen with juice.
In no wise a cowardly, a base fear, a nasty funk
Which claws at the stomach, but a great, but a
    lofty, but a noble fear,
The fear of displeasing me, because he loves me,
    and of disobeying me, because he loves me.
And because he loves me, the fear
Of not being found agreeable
And loving and loved under my gaze. No
    infiltration in that noble fear,
Of an evil funk and of a pernicious and vile
    cowardice.
And when he loves me, it is true. And when he
    says that he loves me, it is true. And when he
    says that he would prefer
To be a leper than to fall into mortal sin (so
    much does he love me), it is true.

When he says it, I know it is true.

It isn't only true that he says it. It is true because
it is true. He doesn't say it because it sounds
well.

He doesn't say that because he saw it in books nor
because someone told him to say it. He says it
because it is so.

He loves me to that extent. He loves me thus.
Freely. A proof of it I have in the same race

And that is the Sire de Joinville (whom I love so
very much, just the same), another French
baron,

Who would on the contrary have committed
thirty mortal sins rather than become a leper.

(Thirty, poor man, how little he knows what he is
talking about)

Doesn't mind saying what he thinks,

That is, saying the opposite

In the presence of even so great a king

And of so great a saint

Whom he nevertheless knew to be such,

That is, displeasing such a great king and such a
great saint. The freedom of speech

Of one who doesn't wish to run the risk

Of being a leper rather than falling into mortal sin,

Insures for me the freedom of speech of him who
prefers being a leper

To falling into mortal sin.

If one says what he thinks, the other too says
what he thinks.

One proves the other . . .
In their rigmarole about leprosy and mortal sin,
    this is how I figure, says God.
When Joinville had rather have committed thirty
    mortal sins than to be a leper,
And when Saint Louis had rather be a leper than
    to fall into one single mortal sin,
I do not conclude, says God, that Saint Louis
    loves me in an ordinary way
And that Joinville loves me thirty times less than
    the ordinary way.
That Saint Louis loves me according to measure, in
    just the wanted measure,
And that Joinville loves me thirty times less than
    the measure.
I reckon, on the contrary, says God, this is how
    I figure, this is how I conclude.
I conclude, on the contrary, that Joinville loves
    me in the ordinary way,
Honestly, just as a poor man is capable of loving me,
Must love me;
And that Saint Louis, on the contrary, loves me
    thirty times above the ordinary,
Thirty times more than honorably;
That Joinville loves me according to measure,
And that Saint Louis loves me thirty times more
    than according to measure.
(And if I put that one in my heaven, at least I
    know why).

That is how I reckon, says God. And so my
     reckoning is fair, because that leprosy which
     they had in mind,
That leprosy of which they talked, and about
     being a leper,
Was anything but an imaginary leprosy and a make
     believe leprosy and an exercise leprosy,
It wasn't a leprosy which they had seen in books
     and heard talked about
More or less vaguely,
It wasn't a leprosy to talk about, nor a leprosy to
     frighten people in conversation and in figures
     of speech,
But this was the real leprosy, and they talked about
     having it themselves, in very sooth,
They knew it well, they had seen it twenty times
In France and in Holy Land,
That disgusting mealy disease, that filthy itch,
     that evil mange,
That repellent scabby disease which makes man
The horror and shame of man,
That ulcer, that dry rot, in a word that definitive
     leprosy
Which eats into the skin and the face and the arm
     and the hand
And the thigh and the leg and the foot
And the stomach and the skin and the bones and
     the nerves and the veins,
That dry white mold which spreads little by little

And bites as if with a mouse's teeth,
And makes a man the refuse and the flight of man,
And destroys a body like a granulous mold,
And grows on the body those awful white lips,
Those awful dry lips of wounds,
And which always advances and never draws back,
And always wins and never loses,
And goes to the end,
And makes of a man a walking corpse.
It was that leprosy they were talking about and
    of none other.
It was that leprosy they had in mind and none
    other,
A real leprosy, in no way a leprosy of exercise.
It was that leprosy which he preferred to have,
    none other.
Well, I think it is thirty times more startling
And that it means loving me thirty times and that
    it means thirty times love.

Ah, to be sure, if Joinville with the eyes of the
    soul had seen
What manner of thing is that leprosy of the soul
Which we not in vain call mortal sin,
If with the eyes of the soul he had seen
That dry rot of the soul infinitely more evil,
Infinitely more ugly, infinitely more pernicious,
Infinitely more malignant, infinitely more odious,

He himself would immediately have understood
how absurd his remark was,
And that the question cannot be raised. But all
do not see with the eyes of the soul.
I understand that, says God. All are not saints, such
is my Christendom.
There are sinners too, there have to be some, it is
thus.
He was a good Christian, nevertheless, all in all,
he was a sinner, there have to be some in
Christendom.
He was a good Frenchman, Jean, sire de Joinville,
a baron of Saint Louis! At least he spoke his
mind.
Those people make up the bulk of the army. There
have to be troops. It is not sufficient to have
leaders who march ahead.
Those people start most honestly on a crusade, at
least once every other time, and very honestly
go on a crusade,
They fight very well and are very properly killed
and win the kingdom of Heaven
Just like any other kingdom . . .
But there you are, they think: I have only one
body (fools, they forget the principal thing,
They forget not only the soul but the body of their
eternity,
The body of the resurrection of the bodies),

Only one body have I, they think (thinking only
    of their earthly body);
If that nasty leprosy takes hold
    of me, I am lost.
(They mean that their temporal body is temporally
    lost) . . .
Now they cling to their body. One would think
    that they believed it was the only thing they
    had.
Yet they know that they have a soul. Life is the
    union of soul and body.
Death lies in their sundering. But their body seems
    to them
A strong and jolly fellow.
They are under the impression that leprosy will
    annihilate their whole body and that it will
    hold them unto the end (they do not consider
    that at the end of that end begins the real
    beginning)
And so they would prefer to have something else
    than leprosy.
I suppose they would prefer to catch
A disease of their liking. It is always the same
    business.
They don't mind facing the most terrible ordeals
And offering me the most awe-inspiring exercises,
So long as they themselves have beforehand
Chosen them. Thereupon the Pharisees cry out
    and exclaim

And shout and make faces, and those execrable
    Pharisees
Above all pray, saying: Lord, we thank Thee
That Thou hast not made us like unto that man
Who feareth to catch leprosy. Now I say, on the
    contrary, says God,
I myself do say: It is something to catch leprosy.
I know what leprosy is. I made it.
I know it. I say: it is something to catch leprosy.
Nor did I ever say that the ordeals and the exercises
    of their lives,
And the diseases and the miseries of their lives,
And the distresses of their lives were nothing.
I have always said, on the contrary, and I have
    always thought
And I have always weighed that it was something,
And indeed it must be believed that it was
    something
Since my Son performed so many miracles on the
    sick
And since I gave the king of France the power
To heal the king's evil.

The Pharisees raise a hue and cry over the one who
    doesn't want to catch leprosy,
And they are scandalized, those virtuous ones.
But I who am not virtuous,
Says God,
I do not shout neither am I scandalized.

I do not figure, I do not conclude that that
    Joinville is thirty times below the ordinary.
But I conclude, but I figure, on the contrary
That it is that Saint Louis who is out of the
    ordinary, thirty times out of the ordinary,
    thirty times extraordinary, thirty times above
    the ordinary.

I do not figure, I do not conclude
That Joinville is thirty times a coward.
But on the contrary, I conclude and I figure
That it is that Saint Louis who is brave thirty
    times,
Brave thirty times above the ordinary and more
    than the measure.

I do not figure, I do not conclude
That Joinville is thirty times lower,
But on the contrary, I conclude and I figure
That it is that Saint Louis who is thirty times
    higher,
Thirty times high above the ordinary and more
    than the measure.

I do not figure, I do not conclude
That Joinville is thirty times small,
But I just know that he is a man.
And on the contrary I conclude and I figure,
This is how I figure,

And it is so.

I conclude and I figure that it is that Saint Louis, king of France,

Who is thirty times great, thirty times above the ordinary and more than the measure.

And who is thirty times close to my heart and thirty times my son's brother.

The Pharisees raise a hue and cry over the one who does not wish to catch leprosy,

But the saint does not raise a hue and cry and is not scandalized.

He knows human nature too well, and man's infirmity, and he is only profoundly grieved.

The Pharisees raise a hue and cry over that man who does not wish to catch leprosy.

See on the contrary how gently the Saint speaks to him,

Firmly but gently.

And that firmness is all the more sure and gives me all the more certainty, all the more assurance and all the more guaranty since it is gentle.

The hearts of sinners are not taken by violence.

They are not pure enough. Only the kingdom of heaven is taken by violence.

INNOCENCE AND EXPERIENCE

God Speaks:

IT IS INNOCENCE that is full and experience
that is empty.
It is innocence that wins and experience that loses.

It is innocence that is young and experience that
is old.
It is innocence that grows and experience that
wanes.

It is innocence that is born and experience that dies.
It is innocence that knows and experience that
does not know.

It is the child who is full and the man who is
empty,
Empty as an empty gourd and as an empty barrel:

That is what I do with that experience of yours.

Now then, children, go to school.
And you men, go to the school of life.

Go and learn
How to unlearn.

All history was enacted twice, says God: once in
    Jewry,
And once in Christendom. The child (Jesus) was
    twice enacted,
Once in Benjamin and once in the child Jesus.
And the lost child and the lost sheep and the lost
    drachma, all were twice enacted.
And the first time, it was in Joseph, *I am Joseph
    your brother*.
It had to be enacted, says God. Twice rather than
    once.
Because there is in the child, there is in childhood
    a unique grace,
An entirety, a firstness
That is total,
An origin, a secret, a spring, a point of departure,
A beginning which might be called absolute.
Children are new creatures.
They too, they in particular, they first among all
    take heaven by force.
Rapiunt, they ravish. But with what sweet
    violence!
And what agreeable force and what tenderness
    of force!
Just as a father willingly submits,
How he loves to submit to the violence of that
    strength!

55

To the embraces of that tenderness!
As for me, says God, I know nothing so beautiful
in the whole world
As a mere child having a talk with the good Lord
At the bottom of the garden;
Asking questions and giving the answers himself
(it's safer that way).
A little man telling the good Lord about his woes,
As seriously as anyone in the world,
And comforting himself as if the good Lord were
comforting him.
But let me tell you that those words of comfort
which he says to himself
Come straight and properly from me.—

Nothing is so beautiful as a child going to sleep
while he is saying his prayers, says God.
I tell you nothing is so beautiful in the world.—
And yet I have seen beautiful sights in the world.
And I know something about it. My creation is
overflowing with beauty.
My creation overflows with marvels.
There are so many that you don't know where to
put them.
I have seen millions and millions of stars rolling
under my feet like the sands of the sea.
I have seen days as scorching as flames,
Summer days of June and July and August.
I have seen winter evenings spread out like a
cloak.

I have seen summer evenings as calm and soft as
    something shed by Paradise,
All studded with stars.
I have seen those slopes of the Meuse and those
    churches which are my own houses,
And Paris and Reims and Rouen and cathedrals
    which are my own palaces and my own
    castles,
So beautiful that I am going to keep them in
    heaven.
I have seen the capital of the kingdom and Rome
    the capital of Christendom.
I have heard mass sung and triumphant vespers.
And I have seen the plains and vales of France,
And they are more beautiful than anything.
I have seen the deep sea, and the deep forest, and
    the deep heart of man.
I have seen hearts devoured by love
During whole lifetimes
Lost in love
Burning like flames.—
I have seen martyrs blazing like torches,
Thus preparing for themselves palms everlastingly
    green.
And I have seen, beading under claws of iron,
Drops of blood which sparkled like diamonds.
And I have seen beading tears of love
Which will last longer than the stars in heaven.
And I have seen looks of prayer, looks of
    tenderness,

Lost in love,
Which will gleam for all eternity, nights and
  nights.
And I have seen whole lives from birth to death,
From baptism to viaticum,
Unrolling like a beautiful skein of wool.
But I tell you, says God, that I know of nothing so
  beautiful in the whole world
As a little child going to sleep while he is saying
  his prayers
Under the wing of his guardian angel
And laughs happily as he watches the angels and
  begins to go to sleep;
And is already mixing his prayers together and no
  longer knows what they are all about;
And sticks the words of *Our Father* among the
  words of *Hail, Mary*, all in a jumble,
While a veil is already coming down over his
  eyelids,
The veil of night over his gaze and over his voice.
I have seen the greatest saints, says God. But I
  tell you
I have never seen anything so funny and I
  therefore know of nothing so beautiful in the
  world
As that child going to sleep while he says his
  prayers
(As that little creature going to sleep in all
  confidence)

And getting his *Our Father* mixed up with his
    Hail, Mary.
Nothing is so beautiful and it is even one point
On which the Blessed Virgin agrees with me—
And I can even say it is the only point on which
    we agree. Because as a rule we disagree,
She being for mercy,
Whereas I, of course, have to be for justice.

The theme of this poem is that beautiful old hymn by Prudentius: Salvete Flores Martyrum, or rather it is a commentary on a few lines from that hymn, the commentary being made with tenderness and humor by God the Father.

THE HOLY INNOCENTS

Nemo poterat dicere canticum, nisi illa centum quadraginta quatuor millia, qui empti sunt de terra.
No man could learn that song but the hundred and forty and four thousand, which were redeemed from the earth. (Apoc. XIV, 3.)

Qui empti sunt de terra. So many others died in my
    Son's name,
In nomine Patris, et Filii, et Spiritus Sancti,
So many died to preserve the honor
Of my Son's name; and they
Who are alone to bear that name on their
    foreheads
And alone can sing that new song,
Are assuredly the only ones on earth
To whom my Son's name was totally unknown.
    Such is my decree.

That name for which they died, they did not
	know,
They never knew it on earth. That is what I like,
	says God.
Now, perhaps, they know it. For ever and ever, it
	can be read
On one hundred and forty-four thousand
	foreheads. On none other.
On not one more. But when they were alive and
	on earth,
One can say that they never knew what people
	were talking about,
Nor even that people were talking, nor that one
	could talk,
(about something). That is what pleases me, says
	God.
Now, they were crying, and laughing, and
	sucking, and screaming, and sleeping.
It was their great, it was their most serious
	occupation.
And a day came
When,
A day (they did not know the name of Herod any
	more than that of Jesus)
(and they did not know the name of Jesus any
	more than that of Herod. I shall venture to say
That they were equally indifferent to both those
	names.) Now both those men,

Jesus, Herod, Herod, Jesus,
Antagonists, were simply going to obtain for them
The glory of my paradise,
The kingdom of heaven and eternal glory. A day
came
When a horde of soldier brutes, attending to their
business
(But exceeding a little its limits, all the same),
An onrush of brutes went by, gendarmes of a kind,
ogres as in fairy tales, bogey men
for children,
Carrying sabres that were like big cutlasses,
And they were Herod's soldiers.
An onrush, a tumult. An uproar; arms with sleeves
rolled up, an outcry.
Shrieks. Teeth. Glistening looks.
Women fleeing, women biting,
Just as they always do when they are not the
strongest;
And there was nothing in the blood and the milk
But a great strewing of dead bodies,
A cemetery of babes and of young Jewish
women.
You know, says God, what we have done with
them.
Those eyes that had hardly opened to the light of
the carnal sun,
Forever and ever were shut to the light of the
carnal sun;

Those eyes that had hardly opened to the light of
the earthly sun
Forever and ever were closed to the light of the
earthly sun;
Those eyes that had hardly opened to the light of
the temporal sun
Forever and ever were closed to the light of the
temporal sun;
Those gazes that had hardly ascended towards the
day and the sun of time
Forever and ever were closed to those transient,
To those perishable lights.
Those voices, those lips that had never sung the
praises of God on earth,
That had never opened but to ask to suck (But so
does it suit me, says God),
Are thus the only ones, are today the only ones,
Are also the only ones that can sing that new song.
Qui empti sunt de terra. You see what we have
done with them, says God.
Let the Innocents' hands be filled. Here is a case in
point. These Innocents had simply picked
up in the scuffle
The kingdom of God and eternal life. What
matter today
Their white limbs broken in the market-towns of
Judea,
And their little dimpled arms cut off as by men
pruning,

And their little fingers stiff and clenched in the
    palms of their hands,
And their cries thrust back into their throats,
    the criminal hands thrusting them back,
    hands crammed in their throats like a stopper,
    like a plug,
And the youthful blood gushing from the heart.
    What matter the severed limbs,
The white thighs like kid's flesh and like the tender
    thighs of little sucking pigs,
And their mothers shrieking like lunatics and biting
    the soldiers' wrists? As in a battle, after the
    battle
The prowlers, the robbers come and rifle the
    wounded and the dead and the dying to take
    away and steal all that is worthwhile.
All that is worth something, novel prowlers, novel
    thieves, those innocents
In that battle, after that battle, rifled themselves
And in the clangor of arms, in the tumult and
    among the shrieks,
In the maddened galloping, in the frenzied pursuit,
    among the women felled to the ground, they
    snatched up all that counts,
They stole all that was worth something, for they
    plundered
Like those who rob corpses and they robbed
    themselves, and what they snatched up in the
    scuffle was no less

Than the kingdom of heaven and eternal life. *Hi
empti sunt ex hominibus.* They alone,
Who alone perhaps on earth not only had never
sung the praises of God,
But had never pronounced even my name nor
my son's name,
They too, only they do not have at the corners of
their mouths that ineffaceable line,
That line of misfortune and ingratitude
And of a bitterness that can never be satiated . . .

Undefiled in the way, thus did John see them,
Upon Mount Sion
Around the standing Lamb. Everything seems to be
for them. *They follow the Lamb
whithersoever He goeth.*
(The greatest saints, apparently, do not follow
him everywhere.)

These were redeemed from among men:
(*from among men, from the midst of men, from
being men*)
The greatest saints have been men, have not been
redeemed from being men.

and in their mouth was found no lie:

for they are spotless before the throne of God.

And the Apostle calls them *primitiae Deo, et*
   Agno: firstfruits to God, and to the Lamb. That
   is to say, the firstfruits of the earth that are
   offered to God and to the Lamb. The other
   saints are the ordinary fruits, the fruits of the
   season. But they are the fruits
Of the very promise of the season.

And following the Apostle, the Church repeats:
   Innocentes pro Christo infantes occisi sunt,

the Innocents for Christ
as children were massacred,

(*infantes*, very young children, very small
   children not yet able to speak);

ab iniquo rege
lactentes interfecti sunt:

by a wicked King
they, sucklings, were massacred:

(*lactentes*, full of milk, milky, at the age of milk,
   being yet on the milk diet,
fed on milk)

ipsum sequuntur Agnum sine macula
they follow the Lamb himself spotless

(and such is the text, my child, that it is at the same
    time the Lamb that is spotless
And they with him who are spotless).

But the Church goes further, the Church goes
    beyond, the Church outstrips the Apostle.

No longer does the Church only say that they are
    the firstfruits to God and to the Lamb,
But the Church invokes them and calls them

flowers of the Martyrs.

Literally meaning by those words that the *other*
    martyrs are the fruits, whereas these, among
    martyrs, are the flowers themselves.

Salvete FLORES *Martyrum:*

Hail, FLOWERS *of Martyrs.*

Laid out on the wooden horse, tied to the wooden
    horse like fruit tied to an espalier,
The other martyrs, twenty centuries of martyrs,
Centuries of centuries of martyrs,
Are literally the fruits of the season,
Of each season arranged at intervals on the
    espalier,

And specially the autumn fruits;
And my son himself was gathered
In his three and thirtieth season. But they, those
simple innocents,
They are before the fruits themselves, they are the
promise of the fruit.
Salvete flores Martyrum, those children less than
two years old are the flowers of all the other
martyrs,
That is to say, the flowers that produce the
other martyrs.
At the very beginning of April, they are the rosy
blossom of the peach tree.
In mid-April, at the very beginning of May, they
are the white blossom of the pear tree.
In mid-May, they are the red blossom of the
apple tree,
White and red.
They are the blossom itself and the bud of the
blossom and the down on the bud.
They are the bourgeon on the twig and the bud
of the blossom.
They are the pride of April and its sweet hope,
They are the pride of the woods and of the
months,
They are little childhood.
The *Reminiscere* Sunday is only for them,
because they remember.

The *Oculi* Sunday is only for them, because they
see.
The *Laetare* Sunday is only for them, because they
rejoice.
Passion Sunday is only for them, because they
were the first Passion.
Palm Sunday is only for them, because they are
the palm itself that bore much fruit.
And Easter Sunday is only for them, because they
are risen again.
They are the flower of the hawthorn that blooms
during holy week.
They are the flower of the blackthorn that blooms
five weeks earlier.
They are the flower of all those plants and of all
those rosaceous trees.
Promise of so many martyrs, they are rosebuds in
a dew of blood.*

Salvete flores Martyrum,
Hail, flowers of Martyrs.

quos, lucis ipso in limine,
Christi insecutor sustulit,

ceu turbo nascentes rosas.

* *An untranslatable pun on rose and rosée (dew). There are*
numerous puns in Péguy's poems; they have well nigh driven
this translator to despair.

69

whom, on the very threshold of light,
Christ's persecutor took away
(carried away)

ceu turbo nascentes rosas.

as a tempest with budding roses.
(that is, as the tempest, as a tempest takes away,
    carries away budding roses)

Vos prima Christi victima,
Grex immolatorum tener,
Aram sub ipsam simplices
Palma et coronis luditis.

Ye, first victim of Christ,
Tender flock of innocents slain
At the foot of the altar itself, simple
Simplices, simple souls, simple children,
Palma et coronis luditis. You play with the palm
    and the crowns. With your palm and your
    crowns.

Such is my paradise, says God. My paradise is
    just as simple as possible.
Nothing is so bare as my paradise.
Aram sub ipsam at the foot of the altar itself
These simple children *play* with their palms and
    with their martyrs' crowns.

70

That is what goes on in my paradise. What game
    can one play
With a palm and with martyrs' crowns?
I suppose they roll hoops, says God, and perhaps
    they play at 'graces,' *
(that is, I think so, for you must not believe
that they ever ask me for my permission),
And the evergreen palm apparently serves as a stick.

* *It is very characteristic of Péguy to end the third of his
Mysteries with a pun; he could never resist a play on words.
Here the reference is to a game played in France forty or fifty
years ago. It was called* jeu de grâces *and required two sticks
about the length of drumsticks, one small hoop and the ability
to throw the hoop towards the sky with the help of the sticks
and catch it again. Ladies excelled at this and their attitudes,
when correct, were deemed worthy of the Graces. Hence the
name, I suppose.*

A VISION OF PRAYER

God Speaks:

I AM THEIR FATHER, says God. *Our Father*
   who art in Heaven. My son told them
   often enough that I was their father.
I am their judge. My son told them so. I am also
   their father.
I am especially their father.
Well, I am their father. He who is a father is above
   all a father. *Our Father who art in Heaven.*
   He who has once been a father can be nothing
   else but a father.
They are my son's brothers; they are my children;
   I am their father.
Our Father who art in Heaven, my son taught
   them that prayer. *Sic ergo vos orabitis.* After
   this manner therefore pray ye.
Our Father who art in Heaven, he knew very well
   what he was doing that day, my son who loved
   them so.
Who lived among them, who was like one of them.
Who went as they did, who spoke as they did,
   who lived as they did.

Who suffered.

Who suffered as they did, who died as they did.

And who loved them so, having known them.

Who brought back to heaven a certain taste for
man, a certain taste for the earth.

My son who loved them so, who loves them
eternally in heaven.

He knew very well what he was doing that day,
my son who loved them so.

When he put that barrier between them and me,
Our Father who art in Heaven, those three or
four words.

That barrier which my anger and perhaps my
justice will never pass.

Blessed is the man who goes to sleep under the
protection of that outpost, the outpost of
those three or four words.

Those words that move ahead of every prayer like
the hands of the suppliant in front of his face.

Like the two joined hands of the suppliant
advancing before his face and the tears of his
face.

Those three or four words that conquer me, the
unconquerable.

And which they cause to go before their distress
like two joined and invincible hands.

Those three or four words which move forward
like a beautiful cutwater fronting a lowly ship.

Cutting the flood of my anger.

And when the cutwater has passed, the ship
    passes, and back of them the whole fleet.
That, actually, is the way I see them, says God;
During my eternity, eternally, says God.
Because of that invention of my Son's, thus must I
    eternally see them.
(And judge them. How do you expect me to
    judge them now.
After that.)
Our Father who art in Heaven, my son knew
    exactly what to do
In order to tie the arms of my justice and untie the
    arms of my mercy.
(I do not mention my anger, which has never
    been anything but my justice.
And sometimes my charity.)
And now I must judge them like a father. As if a
    father were any good as a judge. *A certain*
    man had two sons.
As if he were capable of judging. *A certain man*
    had two sons. We know well enough how
    a father judges. There is a famous example of
    that.

We know well enough how the father judged the
    son who had gone away and came back.
The father wept even more than the son.
That is the story my son has been telling them.
    My son gave them

74

The secret of judgement itself.
And now this is how they seem to me; this is how
    I see them;
This is how I am obliged to see them.
Just as the wake of a beautiful ship grows wider
    and wider until it disappears and loses itself,
But begins with a point, which is the point of the
    ship itself.
So the huge wake of sinners grows wider and wider
    until it disappears and loses itself
But it begins with a point, which is the point of the
    ship itself, and it is that point which comes
    towards me,
Which is turned towards me.
It begins with a point, which is the point of the
    ship itself.
And the ship is my own son, laden with all the sins
    of the world.
And the point of the ship is the two joined hands
    of my son.
And before the look of my anger and the look of
    my justice
They have all hidden behind him.
And all of that huge cortège of prayers, all of that
    huge wake grows wider and wider until it
    disappears and loses itself.
But it begins with a point and it is that point
    which is turned towards me.
Which advances towards me.

And that point is those three or four words: *Our
    Father who art in Heaven;* verily my son
    knew what he was doing.
And every prayer comes up to me hidden behind
    those three or four words.—
Our Father who art in Heaven.—And behind
    (these words) widens until it disappears and
    loses itself
The wake of innumerable prayers
As they are spoken in their text for innumerable
    days
By innumerable men,
(By simple men, his brothers).
Morning prayers, evening prayers;
(Prayers said on all other occasions);
On so many other occasions during innumerable
    days;
Prayers for noon and for the whole day;
Prayers of monks for all hours of the day,
And for the hours of the night;
Laymen's prayers and clerics' prayers
As they were said innumerable times
For innumerable days.
(He spoke like them, he spoke with them, he
    spoke as one of them.)
All of that huge fleet of prayers laden with the sins
    of the world.
All of that huge fleet of prayers and penances
    attacks me
Having the spear you wot of,

Advances towards me having the spear you wot of.
It is a fleet of freighters, *classis oneraria.*
And a fleet of the line,
A combat fleet.
Like a beautiful fleet of yore, like a fleet of
    triremes
Advancing to attack the king.
And what do you expect me to do: I am attacked
And in that fleet, in that innumerable fleet
Each *Our Father* is like a high riding ship
Having itself its own spear, *Our Father who art
    in Heaven*
Turned towards me, and coming behind this
    selfsame spear.
Our Father who art in Heaven, not so smart after
    all. Of course, when a man says that, he can
    get behind what he has said.
When he has said those three or four words.
And behind those beautiful high riding ships, the
    Hail Marys
Advance like innocent galleys, like virginal
    biremes.
Like flat-bottomed boats which do not offend the
    humility of the sea.
Which do not offend the rule, which follow,
    humble and faithful in their submissiveness on
    the surface of the water.
Our Father who art in Heaven. Of course when a
    man begins like that.
When he says those three or four words to me.

When he begins by making those three or four
    words move ahead of him.
After that he can go on, he can tell me what
    he pleases.
Because, you understand, I am disarmed.
And my son knew it well.
My son who loved those men so very much.
Who had acquired a taste for them, and for the
    earth, and all that.
And in this innumerable fleet I clearly distinguish
    three great innumerable fleets.
(I am God, I see well.)
And this is what I see in that huge wake which
    begins with that point and which little by
    little loses itself on the horizon of my gaze.
They are all one behind the other, even those
    which are outside the wake,
Towards my left hand and towards my right hand.
At the head of all of them comes the innumerable
    fleet of *Our Fathers*
Cutting and defying the flood of my anger.
Powerfully seated on three rows of oars.
(That is the way I am attacked. I ask you. Is it
    fair? Is it just?)
(No, it is not just, because all this has to do with
    the reign of my Mercy.)
So, all these sinners and all these saints, walking
    together behind my son.
And behind the joined hands of my son,

And they themselves with joined hands as if they
     were my son.
Well then, my sons. Well then each one a son
     like my son.
First comes the heavy fleet of *Our Fathers*, an
     innumerable fleet.
And in that formation they attack me. I suppose
     you have understood.
The kingdom of heaven suffereth violence, and the
     violent take it by force. They know it well.
     My son told them everything. *Regnum cœli*,
     the kingdom of heaven. Or *regnum cœlorum*,
     the kingdom of heavens.
Regnum cœli vim patitur. Et violenti rapient illud.
     Or *rapiunt.* The kingdom of heaven suffereth
     violence. And the violent take it by force.
     Or will take it by force.
How do you expect me to defend myself? My son
     told them everything. And not only did he do
     that. But he put himself at their head. And
     they are like a great fleet of yore, like an
     innumerable fleet attacking the great king.—

From the high point of my promontory,
The promontory of my justice,
And from the seat of my anger,
And from the chair of my jurisprudence,
In cathedra jurisprudentiae,
From the throne of my eternal greatness

I see coming up towards me, from the far horizon
    I see coming
This fleet which attacks me,
The triangular fleet,
Pointing towards me the spear you wot of.—
And in that innumerable fleet I discover three
    fleets equally innumerable.
And the first is in front, to attack me with greater
    vigor. The high riding fleet,
The ships of powerful hull,
Armored like hoplites,
That is, like soldiers heavily armed.
And they move invincibly ahead, borne on their
    triple rows of oars.

And the first row of oars is:
Hallowed be thy name,
Thy name;

And the second row of oars is:
Thy kingdom come
Thy kingdom;

And the third row of oars is the word
    insurmountable among all words,
Thy will be done on earth as it is in heaven,
Thy will.
Sanctificetur nomen
Tuum.

Adveniat regnum
Tuum.
Fiat voluntas
Tua
Sicut in cœlo et in terra.

And such is the fleet of *Our Fathers*, stalwart and
    more innumerable than the stars in heaven.
    And behind it I see the second fleet, and it is an
    innumerable fleet, for it is the white sailed
    fleet, the innumerable fleet of *Hail Marys*.
And it is a fleet of biremes. And the first row of
    oars is:
Ave Maria, gratia plena;

And the second row of oars is:
Sancta Maria, mater Dei.

And all those *Hail Marys*, and all those prayers of
    the Virgin and the noble *Salve Regina* are
    white caravels, humbly resting under their sails
    on the surface of the water; like white doves
    which one might take with the hand.
Now those sweet doves (resting) under their
    wings,
Those white familiar doves, those doves in one's
    hand,
Those humble doves lying on the surface of the
    hand,

Those doves accustomed to one's hand,
Those caravels vested with sails,
Of all ships are the most opportune,
That is, the ships which present themselves with
	greatest directness in front of the port.

Such is the second fleet, the prayers of the Virgin.
	And the third fleet is made up of the other
	innumerable prayers.
All of them. Those which are said at mass and at
	vespers. And at benediction.
And the prayers of the monks which mark all the
	hours of the day. And the hours of the night.
And the *Benedicite* which is said before sitting
	down to meals.
Before a nice smoking soup-tureen.
All those prayers, all of them. And none are left.

Now I see the fourth fleet. I see the invisible fleet.
	And it is made up of all the prayers which are
	not even said, the words that are not
	even spoken.
But I hear them. Those obscure impulses of the
	heart, the obscure and good impulses, the
	secret good impulses.
Which unconsciously soar up, which are born and
	unconsciously ascend towards me.
And he in whose breast they originate is not even
	aware of them. He doesn't know about
	them, he is only the originator.

But I collect them, says God, and I count them
and weigh them.
Because I am the secret judge.

Such are, says God, these three innumerable fleets.
And the fourth.
These three visible fleets and this fourth invisible
one.
These secret prayers originating in a heart, these
secret prayers of the heart. These secret
impulses.
And being thus assailed with such effrontery,
assailed with prayers and with tears,
Directly assailed, assailed right in the face
After that I am expected to condemn them. How
easy that is!
I am expected to judge them. We know well
enough how all those judgements end up and
all those sentences.
A certain man had two sons. It always ends with
embraces.
(And the father crying even more than anyone
else.)
And with that tenderness which is, which I shall
always put above the Virtues themselves.
Because with its sister Purity it proceeds directly
from the Virgin.

THE PASSION OF OUR LADY

IT WAS THEIR FAULT. It must have been
   their fault.
They had always been too proud of him.
Joseph and she, they had been too proud of him.
It was bound to end badly.
You mustn't be so proud.
You mustn't be as proud as that.—

Weren't they pleased
On the day when that old fellow Simeon
Sang that hymn to the Lord,
Which will be sung forever and ever.
Amen.
And then there was that old woman in the temple.

Weren't they proud!
Too proud.

And that other time too.
The time when he shone among the doctors.
At first they got quite a jolt,

When they came home
And he wasn't with them,
All of a sudden he wasn't with them.
They thought they had forgotten him somewhere.
Mary was all taken aback.
They thought they had lost him.—
That was no joke. It made her tremble.
It wasn't something that happened every day
To lose a twelve-year-old boy.
A big twelve-year-old boy.

Fortunately they found him in the temple in the
    midst of the doctors.
Sitting in the midst of the doctors.
And the doctors listening religiously.
He was teaching, at the age of twelve, he was
    teaching in the midst of the doctors.
How proud they had felt.
Too proud.

Just the same, he ought to have been careful, that
    day.
He had really been too brilliant, he shone too much
    in the midst of the doctors.
Too much for the doctors.
He was too great among the doctors.
For the doctors.
He had let it be seen too clearly.
He had let it be seen too much.

He had made it known too manifestly that he was
　　God.
Doctors don't like that.
He ought to have been more careful. People like
　　that have good memories.
It is even because they have such good memories
　　that they are doctors.
He surely hurt their feelings that day.
And doctors have a good memory.
Doctors have a memory that goes way back.

He ought to have been more careful. Those people
　　have a memory that goes back a good deal.
And then they always stick together.
They uphold each other.
Doctors have a memory that goes way back.
He surely hurt their feelings that day.
When he was twelve.
And when he was thirty-three, they got him.
And this time they wouldn't let him off.
It meant death.
They had him.
They got him.
When he was thirty-three they caught him.
Doctors have a memory that goes way back.—

He had been a good son to his father and mother.
Until the day when he began his mission.—
He was generally liked.

Everybody liked him.
Until the day when he began his mission.
His comrades, his friends, his companions, the
     authorities,
The citizens,
His father and mother,
They all thought what he did was all right.
Until the day when he began his mission.—

The authorities thought what he did was all right.
Until the day when he began his mission.
The authorities considered he was a man of order.
A serious young man.
A quiet young man.
A young man with good habits.
Easy to govern.
Giving back to Caesar what was Caesar's.
Until the day when he had begun disorder.
Introduced disorder.
The greatest disorder in the world.
The greatest there ever was in the world.
The greatest order there had been in the world.
The only order.
There had ever been in the world.—

He was a good son to his father and mother.
He was a good son to his mother Mary.
And his father and mother thought everything
     was all right.

His mother Mary thought it was all right.
She was happy, she was proud of having such a son.
Of being the mother of such a son.—
And she gloried perhaps a little in herself, and
    she magnified God.
Magnificat anima mea.
Dominum.
Et exultavit spiritus meus.
Magnificat. Magnificat.
Until the day when he had begun his mission.—
Perhaps she no longer said *Magnificat* then.
For the last three days she wept.
She wept and wept
As no other woman has ever wept.—
No boy had ever cost his mother so many tears.
No boy had ever made his mother weep as much.
And that is what he had done to his mother
Since he had begun his mission.—

For the past three days she had been wandering,
    and following.
She followed the people.
She followed the events.
She seemed to be following a funeral.
But it was a living man's funeral.—
She followed like a follower.
Like a servant.
Like a weeper at a Roman funeral.—

As if it had been her only occupation.
To weep.—
That is what he had done to his mother.
Since the day when he had begun his mission.—
You saw her everywhere.
With the people and a little apart from the people.
Under the porticoes, under the arcades, in drafty
    places.
In the temples, in the palaces.
In the streets.
In the yards and in the back yards.
And she had also gone up to Calvary.
She too had climbed up Calvary.
A very steep hill.
And she did not even feel that she was walking.
She did not even feel that her feet were carrying
    her.—
She too had gone up *her* Calvary.
She too had gone up and up
In the general confusion, lagging a little
    behind . . .
She wept and wept under a big linen veil.
A big blue veil.
A little faded.—
She wept as it will never be granted to a woman
    to weep.
As it will never be asked
Of a woman to weep on this earth.

Never at any time.—

What was very strange was that everyone respected
    her.

People greatly respect the parents of the
    condemned.

They even said: *Poor woman.*

And at the same time they struck at her son.

Because man is like that.—

The world is like that.

Men are what they are and you never can change
    them.

She did not know that, on the contrary, he had
    come to change man.

That he had come to change the world.

She followed and wept.

And at the same time they were beating her boy.—

She followed and wept.

Everybody respected her.

Everybody pitied her.

They said: *Poor woman.*

Because they weren't perhaps really bad.

They weren't bad at heart.

They fulfilled the Scriptures.—

They honored, respected and admired her grief.

They didn't make her go away, they pushed
    her back only a little

With special attentions

Because she was the mother of the condemned.

They thought: It's the family of the condemned.

They even said so in a low voice.
They said it among themselves
With a secret admiration.—
She followed and wept, and didn't understand
     very well.
But she understood quite well that the government
     was against her boy.
And that is a very bad business.—
She understood that all the governments were
     together against her boy.
The government of the Jews and the government
     of the Romans.
The government of judges and the government
     of priests.
The government of soldiers and the government of
     parsons.
He could never get out of it.
Certainly not.—
What was strange was that all derision was
     heaped on him.
Not on her at all.—
There was only respect for her.
For her grief.—
They didn't insult her.
On the contrary.
People even refrained from looking at her too much.
All the more to respect her.
So she too had gone up.
Gone up with everybody else.

Up to the very top of the hill.
Without even being aware of it.
Her legs had carried her and she did not even
　　　know it.
She too had made the Way of the Cross.
The fourteen stations of the Way of the Cross.
Were there fourteen stations?
Were there really fourteen stations?—
She didn't know for sure.
She couldn't remember.
Yet she had not missed one.
She was sure of that.
But you can always make a mistake.
In moments like that your head swims. . . .
Everybody was against him.
Everybody wanted him to die.
It is strange.
People who are not usually together.
The government and the people.—
That was awful luck.
When you have someone for you and someone
　　　against you, sometimes you can get out of it.
You can scramble out of it.
But he wouldn't.
Certainly he wouldn't.
When you have everyone against you.
But what had he done to everyone?

I'll tell you.
He had saved the world.

HOPE

I AM, says God, Master of the Three Virtues.

Faith is a faithful wife.
Charity is an ardent mother.
But hope is a tiny girl.

I am, says God, the Master of Virtues.

Faith is she who remains steadfast during
    centuries and centuries.
Charity is she who gives herself during centuries
    and centuries.
But my little hope is she
Who rises every morning.

I am, says God, the Lord of Virtues.

Faith is she who remains tense during centuries
    and centuries.
Charity is she who unbends during centuries and
    centuries.
But my little hope
is she who every morning
wishes us good day.

I am, says God, the Lord of Virtues.

Faith is a soldier, a captain holding a fort,
One of the king's cities,
In the borderland of Gascony, in the borderland
    of Lorraine.
Charity is a physician, a little sister of the poor,
Who nurses the sick, who nurses the wounded,
The king's poor,
In the borderland of Gascony, in the borderland
    of Lorraine.
But my little hope is she
Who says how do you do to the poor and to the
    orphan.

I am, says God, the Lord of Virtues.

Faith is a church, a cathedral rooted in the soil
    of France.
Charity is a hospital, an almshouse which gathers
    up all the miseries of the world.
But if it weren't for hope, all that would be nothing
    but a cemetery.

I am, says God, the Lord of Virtues.

Faith is she who watches during centuries and
    centuries.
Charity is she who watches during centuries and
    centuries.

But my little hope is she
who goes to bed every night
and gets up every morning
and really sleeps very well.

I am, says God, the Lord of that virtue.

My little hope is she
who goes to sleep every night,
in that child's crib of hers,
after having said her prayers properly,
and who every morning wakes up and rises
and says her prayers with a new look in her eyes.

I am, says God, Lord of the Three Virtues.

Faith is a great tree, an oak rooted in the heart of
    France.
And under the wings of that tree, Charity, my
    daughter Charity shelters all the woes of the
    world.
And my little hope is nothing but that little earnest
    of a bud which shows itself at the beginning
    of April.
And when one sees the tree, when one looks at
    the oak,
That rough bark of the oak thirteen and fourteen
    hundred years old,
Which will be a centenarian and centuries
    old for centuries and centuries,

That hard, rough bark and those limbs which are
    like a confusion of huge arms,
(A confusion which is an order),
And those roots which thrust into the soil and
    lay hold of it like a confusion of huge legs,
(A confusion which is an order),
When one sees such strength and such roughness,
    the tender little bud no longer seems to
    be anything at all.
It is the bud that looks as if it were the tree's
    parasite, as if it ate at the tree's table,
Like mistletoe, like a mushroom.
It is the bud that looks as if it were getting
    nourishment from the tree (indeed the peasant
    calls them *greedies*), it is the bud that looks as
    if it were resting on the tree, coming out of
    the tree, as if it could not be, as if it could not
    exist without the tree. And today, in truth, it
    comes out of the tree, at the armpit of the
    limbs, at the armpit of the leaves, and it can no
    longer exist without the tree. It looks as if it
    came from the tree, as if it were robbing the tree
    of its sustenance.
And yet it is from that bud, on the contrary, that
    everything comes. Without a bud that once
    appeared, the tree would not exist. Without
    those thousands of buds that come out once
    at the beginning of April and sometimes
    in the last days of March, nothing would last,

the tree would not last and would not keep
its place as a tree (that place must be kept),
without that sap which rises and weeps in
the month of May, without those thousands of
buds that begin to grow tenderly at the
armpits of the hard limbs.
Every place must be kept. All life comes from
tenderness. All life comes from that tender,
delicate April bud and from that sap that
weeps in May, and from the cotton-wool and
the down of that delicate white bud that is clad,
that is warmly, that is tenderly protected by
the tuft of the fleece of a vegetable wool, the
wool of a tree. In that cotton-like tuft lies
the secret of all life. The rough bark looks like
a cuirass in comparison with that tender bud.
But the rough bark is nothing but a hardened
bud, a bud grown old. And that is why the
tender bud always pierces through, always
springs up from under the rough bark.
The toughest warrior was once upon a time a
tender child, a child fed on milk; and the
most rugged martyr, the toughest martyr on
the wooden horse, the martyr with the most
rugged bark, with the roughest skin, the
hardest martyr clawed by talons and nails, was
once upon a time a tender child, a child fed
on milk.
Without that bud which does not look like

anything, which seems as nothing, all that
would be as dead wood.
And the dead wood will be cast into the fire.

Now I tell you, says God, that without that late
April budding, without those thousands of buds,
without that one little budding of hope, which
obviously anyone can break off, without that
tender, cotton-like bud, which the first man
who comes along can snap off with his nail, the
whole of my creation would be nothing but
dead wood.
And the dead wood will be cast into the fire.

And my whole creation would be nothing than a
huge cemetery.
Now my son has told them: *Let the dead bury
their dead.*

Alas my son, alas my son, alas my son;
My son who, on the cross, had a skin as dry as dry
bark;
A withered skin, a wrinkled skin, a tanned skin;
A skin that was split by the nails;
My son had been a tender child, a child fed on milk,
a childhood, a budding, a promise, a pledge;
an attempt, an origin; the beginning of a
redeemer;
a hope of salvation, a hope of redemption.
O day, o evening, o night of the burial,

Fall of that night which I shall never see again,
O night so dear to the heart by what you
	accomplish
And because you are as soothing as balsam,
Night on that mountain and in that valley,
O night, I have so often said that I should not see
	you again,
O night, I shall see you in my eternity.
My will be done. O that time it was that my will
	was done.
Night, I see you still. Three great gallows went
	up, and my son in the middle.
A hill, a valley. They had gone up from that city
	which I had given to my people. They
	had gone up.
My son between those two thieves. One wound in
	his side. Two wounds in his hands. Two
	wounds in his feet. Wounds on his forehead.
Women who wept as they stood. And that leaning
	head, bowed upon his breast.
And that poor dirty beard, all sullied with dust
	and blood,
That red beard with two points,
And that sullied hair, all disordered, which I
	would have kissed so often,
That beautiful red hair, still wet with blood from
	the crown of thorns,
All sullied, all clotted with blood. All was
	fulfilled.
He had borne too much.

That head which leaned forward, which I should
    have placed on my breast,
That shoulder which I should have placed against
    my shoulder,
And that heart no longer beating which had so long
    beaten with love.
Three or four women who wept as they stood.
    As for the men, I don't remember, I don't
    think there were any more.
Perhaps they had thought it was too much of a
    climb. All was over. All was consummated. It
    was the end.
And the soldiers went away, and in their rounded
    shoulders they carried away the Roman might.
It was then, o night, that you came. O night,
    the same
The same that comes every evening and that had
    come so many times since the primeval
    darkness,
The same that descended on Abel's smoking altar
    and on Abel's dead body, on that mangled
    body, on the first murder committed in the
    world.
O selfsame night, you descended on the lacerated
    body, on the first, on the greatest murder in
    the world. It was then, o night, that you came.
The same that had descended on so many
    crimes since the beginning of the world,
And on so many stains and on so much bitterness,

And on that sea of ingratitude, you were the
    same that descended on my grief.
And on that hill and in that valley of my desolation,
    it was then, o night, that you came.
O night, will it then have to be, will it have to be
    that my paradise
Be nought but a great transparent night falling
    on the sins of the world?
Will it be thus, o night, that you will come?
It was then, o night, that you came, and you alone
    were able to finish, you alone were able to
    fulfill that day among days.
Just as you fulfilled that day, o night, you will
    fulfill the world,
And my paradise will be a great luminous night,
And all I shall have to offer
In my offering, I too, in my offertory,
To so many martyrs and to so many tortioners,
To so many souls and to so many bodies,
To so many undefiled and to so many who are
    defiled,
To so many sinners and to so many saints,
To so many faithful and to so many penitents,
And to so many sorrows, and to so many
    bereavements, and to so many tears, and to so
    many wounds,
And to so much blood,
And to so many hearts that have beaten so long
With love, with hatred,

And to so many hearts that have bled so long
With love, with hatred,
Shall it be said that it must be,
And that I shall perforce have to offer,
And that they will not ask any more than that,
That they will desire no more than that,
That they will not relish anything else but that,
On those stains and on so much bitterness,
And on that boundless sea of ingratitude
The slow descending of a night eternal.
O night, you did not have to go and ask Pilate's
    permission. That is why I love and greet you,
And glorify you among all, and among all you
    glorify me,
And do me honor and glory . . .
I am, says God, the Lord of virtues.
Faith is the sanctuary lamp
That burns forever.
Charity is that big, beautiful log fire
That you light in your hearth
So that my children the poor may come and warm
    themselves before it on winter evenings.
And all around Faith, I see all my faithful
Kneeling together in the same attitude, and with
    one voice
Uttering the same prayer.
And around Charity, I see all my poor
Sitting in a circle around that fire

And holding out their palms to the heat of the
    hearth.
But my hope is the bloom, and the fruit, and the
    leaf, and the limb,
And the twig, and the shoot, and the seed, and the
    bud.
Hope is the shoot, and the bud of the bloom
Of eternity itself.

Night

This poem might be described as one of the greatest moments of contemporary French poetry, and indeed of all French poetry. Péguy is here at his best. He is now a complete master of the language, that is, not content with obeying its laws, he compels it to follow him in all the intricacies of his thought and to express what, I believe, had never been said before him. He has subdued it as the magician in the Arabian Nights subdues a genie. Péguy's French is so intensely his own that no one can use it after him without openly declaring himself a thief. There is much to be said about Péguy's grammar. At times, it is peculiar. I do not mean that it is uncertain. Péguy knew all the vast resources of grammar. He knew his grammar as only a Frenchman knows it who has studied Latin, French being little else than Latin continued, as Remy de Gourmont called it, Latin brought into Gaul by soldiers and merchants and thriving there until it became not another tongue, but Latin of another time. Quite often, however, Péguy's grammar goes wild, just as Blake's went wild, under the pressure of inspiration, and his syntax seems simply to burst asunder. He insists on the language saying things it has never said, and the language obeys, not without some awful stutterings. An example of this is the expression pour toujours, *which means, simply: forever. But forever, in the mouth of God the Father, does not seem adequate to Péguy. He wants more eternity in that phrase, so, instead of saying forever, God the Father says, in spite of grammar, in spite of usage, in spite of generations of professors: for eternally.*

Another of Péguy's characteristics is his inordinate love of puns. Not puns as jokes, not puns in the child-like manner of Charles Lamb, but serious puns, almost sacred puns. There are many such puns in the poem on night. Some have almost disappeared in the translation, but they never mar the beauty of the poem. Péguy who did everything in all seriousness, Péguy who proudly asserted that there was not one mortal sin in any of his books, Péguy raised the pun to a level which it had almost never known, I say almost because there is in the Gospels a most solemn and fundamental play on words.

NIGHT

God Speaks:

NIGHTS FOLLOW EACH OTHER and are linked,
   and for the child nights are continuous and
   are the innermost part of his very being.
Therein does he fall back. They are the innermost
   part of his life,
They are his very being. Night is the place, night
   is the being wherein he bathes, and is
   nourished, and is created, and is made,
Wherein he accomplishes his being,
Wherein he recovers his strength.
Night is the place, night is the being wherein he
   rests, wherein he retires, wherein he collects
   himself,
Wherein he enters again. And he comes out
   refreshed. Night is my most beautiful creation.
Now why doesn't man make use of it. I am told
   that there are men who don't sleep at night.
Night, for my children and for my young
Hope, is what it really is. It is the children who see
   and who know. It is my young hope
Who sees and who knows. Who knows what
   being means,

What the being called night is. Night it is that
    continues.
Children know very well. Children see very well.
And it is the days that are discontinuous. It is
    the days that pierce, that disrupt night,
And in no wise the nights that interrupt day.
It is day that troubles night with its noise,
Otherwise night would sleep.
And the solitude, and the silence of night is so
    beautiful and so great
That it surrounds and corners and buries the days
    themselves,
That it makes an august enclosure around the
    restlessness of days.
Children are right, my little hope is right. All
    nights together
Meet and join as in a beautiful roundelay, as in a
    beautiful dance,
A dance of nights holding each other by the hand,
    whereas lean days
Make nothing more than a procession in which
    hands are not joined.
Children are right, my little Hope is right. Nights
    all together
Meet and join above the borders of days, hold out
    their hands to each other
Above the days, form a chain and more than a
    chain,
A roundelay, a dance, nights grasp each other's
    hands

Above the day, from morn till eve,
From the border of morn to the border of eve,
     leaning one towards the other,
The one coming down from the preceding day,
     leans back;
The one going up
To the next day,
Leans forward,
And both join, join hands,
Join their silence and their shadow,
And their piety and their august solitude,
Above the difficult borders,
Above the borders of hard working day.
And all together, thus holding hands,
Overlapping the borders, wrists tied
To wrists, all the nights, one after another,
Together constitute night, and the days, one after
     another,
Together do not constitute day. For they are
     nought but lean days
That do not join hands. Now, just as life,
Earthly life,
In a big, general way (if I may say), is only a
     passage between two borders,
An opening between the night before and the
     night after,
A day,
An opening between the night of darkness and the
     night of light,

So, in a small way, each day is only an opening.
A day.
Not only between the night before and the night
    after,
Between the borders,
But as children see it, as children sense it, and my
    young Hope too, just as children know it,
In the night, in one and the same,
In one and the same night,
Where being recruits itself,
Deep in the night,
It is night that is continuous, wherein being
    recruits itself, it is night that forms one long,
    continuous texture,
An endless continuous texture wherein days are
    nothing but days,*
Opening only like days,
That is, like holes, in a stuff where there is open
    work,
In a stuff, in an open-work texture.
It is night that is my great black wall,
Where days open only like windows
With a restless and flickering
And perhaps a false light,
Where days open only like days,
Where days open only like attic windows;
For it must not be said that the chain of times

* *A play on* jour *meaning an aperture in an open-work stuff*
and jour *meaning day.*

Is comparable to an endless chain
In which link follows link, in which ring follows
ring,
And days and nights are equal and follow each
other in the same chain,
One white ring, one black ring, night hooking on
to day, day hooking on to night,
For they are not equal, they do not share the same
dignity in that chain.
It is night that is continuous. It is night that
forms the texture
Of time, the store of being,
And day looks out on that only through wretched
windows and posterns.
It is day that disrupts, and day looks out on that
Only through sorry
Borrowed lights.* It is day that rends, and days
are like isles in the sea,
Like interrupted isles that interrupt the sea,
But the sea continues and it is the isles that are
wrong.
In the same way, the days are wrong, and
interrupted they interrupt night.
But no matter what they do, they themselves
Are immersed in the night.

* One of Péguy's numerous plays on words. The French
jour de soufrance may mean borrowed light as well as day of
suffering.

Just as the sea is the water supply, so is night the
	reserve of being.
It is time which I have reserved for myself. All
	those feverish days try in vain:
As on the high seas, right in the middle of night,
	they are immersed in the depth of night.
It is they that are dispersed, they that are broken up.
Days are scattered bodies, night is the open sea
In which Saint Paul sailed,
And the border that comes down from night
	towards day
Is always an ascending border,
An abrupt border, and the border that re-ascends
	from day towards night
Is always a descending border, in the depth of
	night.
O night, my most beautiful invention, my creation
	august among all,
My most beautiful creature, creature of the
	greatest Hope,
Giving most substance to Hope,
You who are the instrument, who are the very
	substance and abode of Hope,
And also, (and thus), are really the creature of
	greatest Charity,
For it is you who rock all Creation to sleep,
A refreshing sleep,
Just as one puts a child in his little bed,

Just as his mother puts him to bed, just as his
    mother tucks him in
And kisses him (She is not afraid of waking him.
He sleeps so soundly),
Just as his mother tucks him in and laughs and
    kisses him on the brow,
Enjoying it,
And he too laughs, he laughs in response as he
    sleeps;
Thus, o night, black-eyed mother, universal
    mother,
Not only mother of children (that is so easy),
But mother of men themselves and of women,
    which is so difficult,
It is you, night, who put to bed and make all
    Creation lie down
In a bed of a few hours
(in the mean time), in a bed of a few hours,
An image, a feeble image, and a promise and a
    realisation beforehand of the bed of all the
    hours,
An anticipated realisation, a promise held in
    advance,
While waiting for the bed of all hours,
In which I, the Father, will put my creation.
O Night, you are the night. And all those days
    together
Are never the day, they are never anything but
    days,

Sown. Those days are never anything but lights,
Uncertain lights, and you, night, you are my
    great dark light.
I congratulate myself on having made night.
    Days are islets and isles
That pierce and rend the sea,
But they have to rest in the deep sea,
They are compelled to do so.
Thus, you, days, are compelled,
You have to rest in the deep night,
And you, night, are the deep sea
In which Saint Paul sailed, no longer that little
    lake of Tiberias.
All those days are never anything but limbs
Dismembered. It is the days that emerge, but they
    have to be fixed in deep water,
In deep night. Night, my most beautiful invention,
    it is you who calm, it is you who soothe, it
    is you who put to rest
The aching limbs
All disjointed by the day's work.
It is you who calm, it is you who soothe, it is
    you who put to rest
The aching hearts,
The bruised bodies, the limbs bruised by toil, the
    hearts bruised by toil
And by trouble and daily care.
O Night, o my daughter Night, the most
    religious of my daughters,

The most pious;
Of all my daughters, of all my creatures, you
    are the one who is most in my hands, the one
    who most completely yields;
You glorify me in Sleep even more than your
    Brother Day glorifies me in Work,
For in work, man glorifies me only by his work,
And in sleep, it is I who glorify myself by the
    yielding of man,
And it is safer, I know better how to manage that.
Night, you are for man a food more nourishing
    than bread and wine,
For if he who eats and drinks does not sleep, he will
    derive no benefit from his food,
It will turn to sourness and make him sick;
But if he sleeps, bread and wine will become his
    flesh and blood,
To work, to pray, to sleep.
Night, you are the only one who dress wounds,
Aching hearts, all disjointed, all dismembered.
O my black-eyed daughter, you alone among my
    daughters who are, who can call yourself my
    accomplice,
Who acts in complicity with me, for you and I,
    I through you,
Together we cause man to fall in the snare of my
    arms
And take him somewhat by surprise,
But one takes him as best one can. If someone
    knows that, it is I.

Night, you are a beautiful invention
Of my wisdom.
Night, o my daughter Night, o my silent daughter,
At Rebecca's well, at the Samaritan woman's well,
It is you who draw the deepest water
From the deepest well;
O night, you who put all creatures to sleep,
A refreshing sleep,
O night, you who wash all wounds
In the only fresh water, in the only deep water,
At Rebecca's well, drawn from the deepest well;
Friend of children, friend and sister of young Hope,
O night, you who dress all wounds,
You who, at the Samaritan woman's well, draw
     from the deepest well
The deepest prayer,
O night, o my daughter Night, you who know how
     to hold your peace, o my daughter of the
     beautiful mantle,
You who shed rest and oblivion, you who shed
     balm, and silence, and darkness,
O my starry Night, I created you first.
You who put to sleep, you who, already, in an
     eternal Darkness bury
All my creatures,
The most restless, the spirited horse, the hard-
     working ant,
And man, that monster of restlessness,
Night, you who succeed in putting to sleep man,
That well of restlessness,

More restless in himself than all creation put
     together,
Man, that well of restlessness,
Just as you put to sleep the water in the well.
O my night of the long robe,
You who gather children and young Hope
In the folds of your robe,
But men won't allow themselves to be treated
     thus,
O my beautiful night, I created you first,
And almost before that,
Silent one of the long veils,
You by whom there comes down on earth a
     foretaste,
You who spread with your hands, you who shed on
     earth
A first peace,
     Fore-runner of eternal peace,
A first rest,
     Fore-runner of eternal rest,
A first balm, so cool, a first beatitude,
     Fore-runner of eternal beatitude,
You who soothe, you who smell sweet, you who
     comfort,
You who dress wounds and bruised limbs,
You who put hearts to sleep, you who put bodies
     to sleep,
Aching hearts, aching bodies,
Bodies all stiff,

Limbs overwhelmed with fatigue, backs broken
with weariness,
With tiredness, with cares, with restlessness,
Mortal restlessness,
With troubles,
You who shed balm on throats rent by bitterness,
Such a cool balm,
O my daughter of the great heart, I created you
first,
Almost before the first, my daughter of the
limitless bosom,
And well I knew what I was doing,
Perchance I knew what I was about;
You who lay the child in his mother's arms,
The child suffused with light by a shadow of
sleep,
All laughter within himself, secretly laughing
because of his confidence in his mother
And in me,
Secretly laughing with a serious pucker of his lips,
You who lay the child that is replete and
overflowing with innocence
And confidence,
In his mother's arms.
You who lay the child Jesus every evening
In the arms of the Very Holy and Immaculate one,
You who are the portress of Hope,
O my daughter, first among all, you who succeed
even, in this,

You who sometimes succeed, in this,
You who lay man in the arms of my Providence,
My maternal Providence,
O my *dark and gleaming* daughter, I greet you,
You who restore, you who nourish, you who rest,
O silence of darkness,
Such a silence reigned before the creation of unrest,
Before the beginning of the reign of unrest,
Such a silence will reign, but it will be a silence of
 light,
When all that unrest is brought to an end,
When all that unrest is exhausted,
When they have drawn all the water from the well,
After the end, after the exhaustion of all that
 unrest
Of man.
Thus, daughter, you are ancient and you are late,
For in this reign of unrest, you call to mind, you
 commemorate, you almost establish anew,
You almost cause to begin again the former
 Quietude
When my spirit moved upon the face of the
 waters.
But also, my starry daughter, daughter of the dark
 mantle, you are very much ahead of time, you
 are very precocious,
For you announce, for you represent, you almost
 cause to begin, ahead of time, every evening,
My great Quietude of light,
Of eternal light.

Night, you are holy, Night, you are great, Night,
     you are beautiful,
Night of the great mantle.
Night, I love you and greet you, and I glorify you,
     and you are my big daughter and my creature.
O beautiful night, night of the great mantle,
     daughter of the starry mantle,
You remind me, even me, you remind me of that
     great silence there was
Before I had opened up the floodgates of
     ingratitude,
And you announce to me, even me, you announce
     the great silence there will be
When I will have closed them.
O sweet, o great, o holy, o beautiful night, perhaps
     the holiest of my daughters, night of the long
     robe, of the starry robe,
You remind me of that great silence there was in
     the world
Before the beginning of the reign of man.
You announce to me that great silence there will be
After the end of the reign of man, when I will
     have resumed my scepter.
And at times I think of it beforehand, for that
     man really makes a lot of noise.
But specially, Night, you remind me of that night,
And I shall remember it eternally:
The ninth hour had struck. It was in the land of
     my people Israel.
All was over. That enormous adventure.

From the sixth hour, there had been darkness over
    all the land until the ninth hour.
All was over. Let us not mention it any more. It
    hurts me.
That unbelievable coming down of my son among
    men,
In the midst of men,
When you think what they made of it,
Those thirty years during which he was a carpenter
    among men,
Those three years during which he was a kind of
    preacher among men,
A priest,
Those three days during which he was a victim
    among men,
In the midst of men,
Those three nights during which he was a dead
    man among men,
In the midst of dead men,
Those centuries and centuries when he is a host
    among men.
All was over, that unbelievable adventure
By which I, God, have tied my arms for my
    eternity,
The adventure by which my Son tied my arms,
For eternally tying the arms of my justice, for
    eternally untying the arms of my mercy,
And against my justice inventing a new justice,
A justice of love, a justice of Hope. All was over.

That which was necessary. In the way that was
    necessary. In the way my prophets had
    announced it. The veil of the temple was rent
    in twain from top to bottom;
The earth did quake; the rocks rent;
The graves were opened; and many of the bodies
    of the saints which slept arose.
And about the ninth hour, my Son uttered
The cry that will never be still. All was over. The
    soldiers returned to their barracks,
Laughing and joking because that duty was over,
One more guard duty they would not have to
    stand.
Only one centurion remained, with a few men,
A very small post to guard that unimportant
    gallows,
The gallows on which my Son was hanged.
A few women only had remained.
The Mother was there.
And perhaps a few disciples too, and even so, one
    is not sure of that.
Now every man has the right to bury his son,
Every man on earth, if he has had that great
    misfortune
Not to have died before his son. And I alone, I,
    God,
Arms tied by that adventure,
I alone, at that moment, father after so many
    fathers,

I alone could not bury my son.

It was then, o night, that you came,

O my daughter, beloved among all, and I still see it, and I shall see that in my eternity.

It was then, o Night, that you came, and in a great shroud you buried

The centurion and his Romans,

The Virgin and the holy women,

And that mountain, and that valley on which evening was descending,

And my people Israel and the sinners, and together him who was dying, who had died for them,

And the men of Joseph of Arimathea who already were approaching,

Bearing the white shroud.

EDITOR'S NOTE

The title and subtitles are not Péguy's. Omissions in the text are indicated by dashes. The whole text is quoted from Charles Péguy's 'Cahiers de la Quinzaine,' Paris 1900–1914. Therefore the dates of quotations refer to their first publication. The roman numerals indicate the Series numbers of the 'Cahiers,' the arabic numerals indicate the number of the issue. Spelling and punctuation correspond to the text of the 'Cahiers.'

SOURCES

Sleep	*La Deuxième Vertu*	XIII,	4	1911
Abandonment	*Saints Innocents*	XIII,	12	1912
Freedom	*Saints Innocents*	XIII,	12	1912
Mortal Sin . . .	*Saints Innocents*	XIII,	12	1912
Innocence . . .	*Saints Innocents*	XIII,	12	1912
The Holy Innocents	*Saints Innocents*	XIII,	12	1912
A Vision of Prayer	*Saints Innocents*	XIII,	12	1912
The Passion of Our Lady	*Jeanne d'Arc*	XI,	6	1910
Hope	*Saints Innocents*	XIII,	12	1912
Night	*La Deuxième Vertu*	XIII,	4	1911